# Air

## Andrew Charman

**Watts Books**
London • New York • Sydney

© 1993 Watts Books

Watts Books
96 Leonard Street
London EC2A 4RH

Franklin Watts Australia
14 Mars Road
Lane Cove
NSW 2066

UK ISBN: 0 7496 1119 7

10  9  8  7  6  5  4  3  2  1

Series editor: Pippa Pollard
Editor: Claire Llewellyn
Design: Shaun Barlow
Cover design: Edward Kinsey
Artwork: Shaun Campbell
Cover artwork: Hugh Dixon
Picture research: Ambreen Husain

Educational advisor: Joy Richardson

A CIP catalogue record for this book
is available from the British Library

Printed in Italy by G. Canale & C. SpA

# Contents

# Air all around us

Air is all around us. We cannot see it or smell it unless it is mixed with other substances. The layer of air which covers planet Earth is called the **atmosphere**. This layer traps a lot of the heat from the earth that would otherwise go back into space. This keeps us warm. Nearly all living things need air to survive. They cannot live without it.

▽ The atmosphere fades into space about 500 kilometres above the earth.

# What is air?

The air that surrounds us is a mixture of **gases**. **Oxygen** and nitrogen make up a large part. There are small amounts of **carbon dioxide** and other gases. Air also contains **water vapour**. This cools to form collections of water droplets called clouds.

  The air gets thinner the higher up you go. It becomes difficult to breathe.

▷ High up on a mountain there is less oxygen in the air. This climber has his own supply.

▷ As the air cools, water vapour changes into tiny droplets of water. They form clouds and eventually fall as rain.

# Air for life

Nearly all the plants and animals on earth need air to survive. It is the oxygen in air that we need. Oxygen travels round our bodies in our **blood**. It helps to break down the food in our **cells** to give us energy. This process makes a gas called carbon dioxide. The air we breathe out contains carbon dioxide and water vapour.

▷ Active bodies need lots of oxygen. This is why athletes breathe heavily when they run.

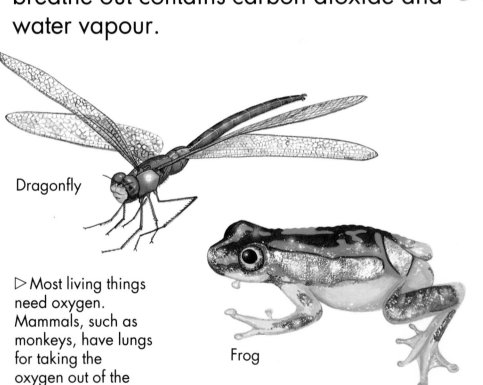

Dragonfly

Frog

Snake

▷ Most living things need oxygen. Mammals, such as monkeys, have lungs for taking the oxygen out of the air. Other animals have different ways of getting oxygen.

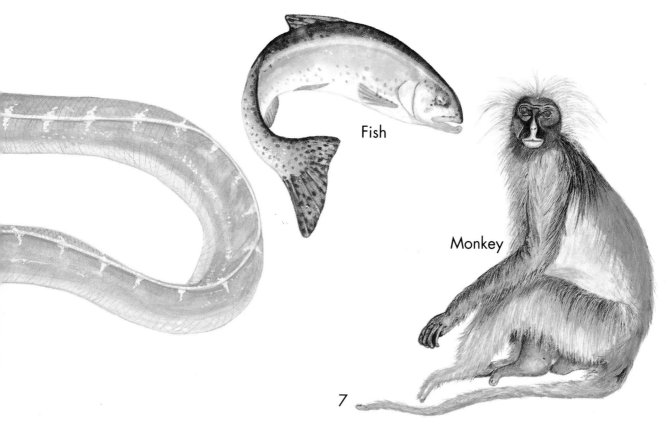

Fish

Monkey

7

# Plants and air

Like animals, plants take in oxygen and use it to break down their food. They are also able to make more oxygen. During daylight hours, green plants take in carbon dioxide. This reacts with water in their leaves and makes food for the plant. Oxygen is given off at the same time. This process is called **photosynthesis**.

▷ Green plants take in carbon dioxide from the air and release oxygen. Most living things depend on this oxygen.

Sunlight

Oxygen

Carbon dioxide

Water

▷ Phytoplankton are tiny plants floating in the sea. These plants make a lot of oxygen.

▽ Forests make huge amounts of oxygen, but many of them are being cut down.

# Air and water

Animals that live in water also need air to breathe. Whales and dolphins are mammals and have lungs like us. They have to come to the surface for air. There is oxygen in water. Fish can take oxygen out of the water with their **gills**. The oxygen is constantly replaced by water-living plants.

▽ Mammals cannot breathe under water. This diver has a supply of oxygen in the air tanks on her back.

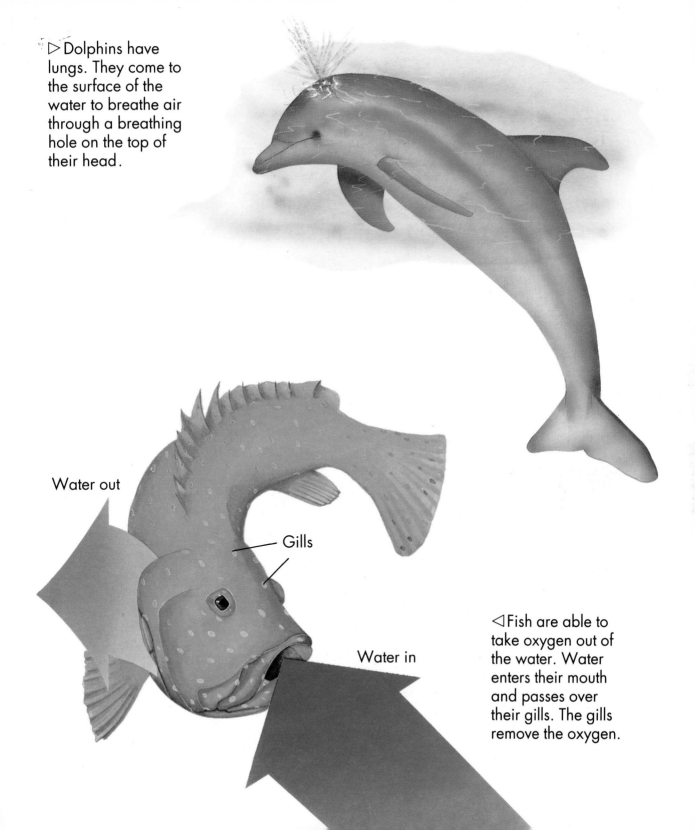

▷ Dolphins have lungs. They come to the surface of the water to breathe air through a breathing hole on the top of their head.

Water out

Gills

Water in

◁ Fish are able to take oxygen out of the water. Water enters their mouth and passes over their gills. The gills remove the oxygen.

# Air pressure

The air in the atmosphere is heavy. It pushes down on us. This is what we call **air pressure**. When air is cold it exerts more pressure than when it is warm. Air will rush from an area of high pressure to one where it is low. This causes winds. Air spreads out to fill the space it is in. It can also be forced into a small space. This gives it high pressure.

▷ Strong winds can sometimes spin. When this happens they form hurricanes or cyclones. This picture of a hurricane was taken from a satellite above the earth.

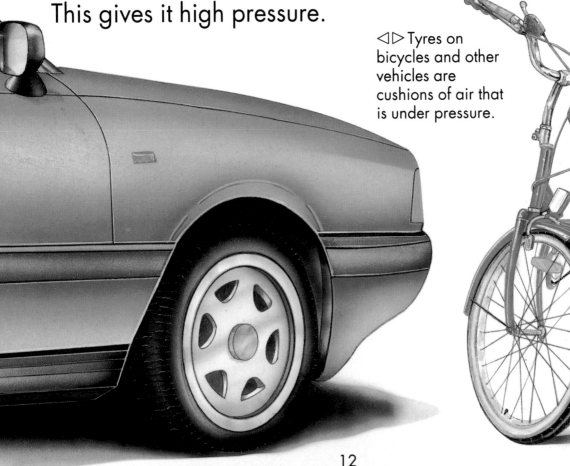

◁▷ Tyres on bicycles and other vehicles are cushions of air that is under pressure.

# Air and the weather

In some parts of the world it is hot and wet. The sun heats the oceans and water vapour rises into the air. Higher up, the air cools and the water falls as rain. Hot desert areas have very little rain. The air above them has little water vapour and rarely cools enough to make clouds. In **polar lands** it is so cold that the water freezes in the clouds. It falls as snow.

▷ When the air is very cold, ice crystals form in the clouds and fall as snow.

▽ Some parts of the world have rainy seasons, when it rains at the same time every day.

▷ Hot deserts have
very little rainfall.
The air does not
hold very much
water vapour.

# Hot air

When air warms up it expands, or gets larger, and takes up more space. This makes it less dense than cold air. Being less dense makes the warm air rise. Air **currents** are rising all the time. The sun heats the earth. Warm air rises from the surface, and cooler air moves in to replace it. Hot air balloons rise in a similar way.

▷ The air inside a hot air balloon is heated by flames from below. This is what makes it rise into the air.

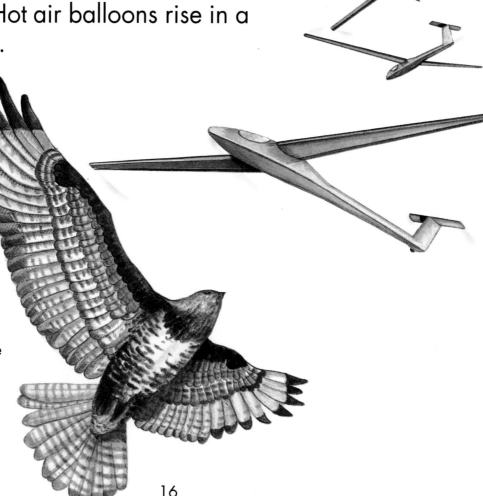

▷ Gliders and gliding birds can climb higher in the air on rising air currents.

16

# Wings and sails

Planes stay in the air because of air pressure. Their wings have a special shape called an **aerofoil**. This makes the air move faster over the top of the wing than it does below. The slow-moving air exerts more pressure than the fast-moving air, and it lifts the plane up into the air. Air passes over a bird's wing in the same way.

▽ A plane must be moving quite fast before there is enough pressure below its wings to lift it into the air.

▷ The sail of a modern sailing boat is shaped like an aerofoil. Wind from the side pushes the boat forwards.

▷ Some racing cars have aerofoils. These work like upside-down wings. They push the car down so that it will stay on the track.

# Air resists

Air resists things. It pushes against them. This is what makes a parachute fall to the ground slowly. It is moving air, or wind, pushing against a sail from behind which makes a boat go along. Huge sailing ships were once used for trade and warfare. Some of them had as many as 40 large sails. Today, most boats are smaller and have only one or two sails.

▷ This modern tanker has two large sails as well as engines. This helps it to save fuel.

◁ Sailing ships of the past relied heavily on the wind behind them to push them along.

▽ Air pushes against an open parachute. This is why the parachutist comes down slowly.

# Energy from air

Moving air will push against the sails of a windmill, making them turn. The energy of the wind is passed on to the turning sails. In the past, this moving energy was used to grind grain or pump water. Modern windmills or **wind turbines** are used to make electricity.

▷ Wind farms have hundreds of wind turbines. They make electricity for many homes.

▽ The first windmills were used about a thousand years ago. They are still used to grind grain into flour.

# Air and sound

Some musical instruments use air to make their sound. Inside a flute or a recorder there is a hollow space. Air **vibrates** inside the space when you blow into the instrument. This means that the tiny particles which make up the air go back and forth very quickly. The vibration is what makes the sound. The sound travels through the air to our ears.

▷ Lightning heats the air around it. The air expands quickly and makes the sound we call thunder.

▷ The air inside a flute vibrates when you blow into it. This makes the sound. Opening and closing the holes changes the note produced.

▷ The air inside a
whistle also vibrates
to make a sound. It
will only produce
one note.

# Polluting the air

When we burn fuels such as coal and oil, gases pass into the air. Too much of these gases can be harmful to people, wildlife and the planet. This is what we mean by **pollution**. We burn fuels to make electricity, to make the things we buy and to run vehicles. Some people believe that we need to use less of these fuels and find different kinds of energy.

▷ Fumes from cars and factories have polluted the air above this city.

▽ Modern cars can run on lead-free petrol. This causes less pollution than ordinary petrol.

▷ Many power
stations burn coal to
make electricity.
Their smoke pollutes
the air.

# Heating up the air

Some of the gases we put into the atmosphere are making our planet warmer. This is called **global warming**. Even a small rise in temperature could be disastrous. Ice at the poles would melt, causing flooding in some areas. The heat would also make the deserts spread. The world's forests help to keep our air clean. We must protect them.

▷ In some parts of the world people are planting new forests. These will help to clean our air.

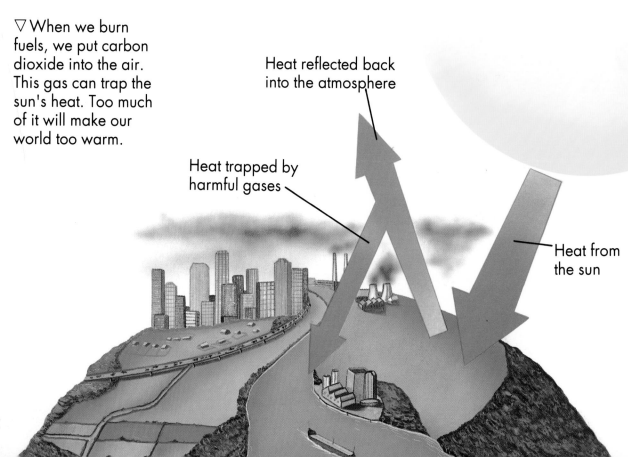

▽ When we burn fuels, we put carbon dioxide into the air. This gas can trap the sun's heat. Too much of it will make our world too warm.

Heat reflected back into the atmosphere

Heat trapped by harmful gases

Heat from the sun

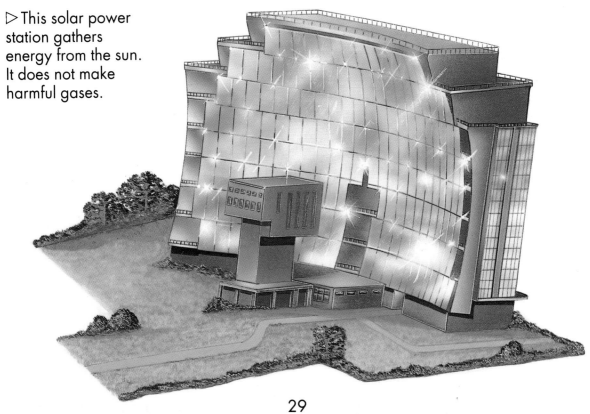

▷ This solar power station gathers energy from the sun. It does not make harmful gases.

# Things to do

- You can use the wind to have fun, like when you fly a kite or sail a model boat. Make a blow-football game. All you need is two straws, a table-tennis ball and lots of puff.

- Find out about the Beaufort wind scale. This is used to describe the strength of the wind. Then you can make a diary of what the wind is like every day for a week.

- Make a wind chime. Cut six pieces of string about 60 cm long. Tie some small objects, such as buttons, bottle tops and beads on to the string. Tape the top end of each piece on to a coat hanger so that the objects can touch each other. Hang your wind chime near a window.

# Glossary

**aerofoil** A wing or other object which has a special curved shape, helping to lift it into or through the air.

**air pressure** The air in the atmosphere exerts a pressure. It pushes down on us.

**atmosphere** The layer of air which surrounds the earth.

**blood** A liquid found inside the bodies of many animals. It carries food materials, waste products and oxygen around the body.

**carbon dioxide** The gas which animals breathe out and which is given off when fuel is burned.

**cells** The tiny units of which all living things are made.

**current** A movement of air, water or electricity.

**gas** A material that is not liquid or solid is a gas.

**gills** The parts of the body used by many water-living animals to take oxygen out of the water.

**global warming** The damaging effect of too many harmful gases in the air. They are making our world too warm.

**lungs** The parts of the body used by animals who take their oxygen from the air.

**oxygen** The gas that nearly all living things need to survive.

**photosynthesis** The making of food by green plants.

**polar lands** The two very cold areas at the northern and southern ends of the earth.

**pollution** The damaging effect of too many harmful materials in water, air or earth.

**vibrate** To move back and forth very quickly.

**water vapour** Water in the form of a gas.

**wind turbine** A machine which turns the movement of the wind into mechanical energy.

# Index

**Photographic credits:** Austin J. Brown 18; Eye Ubiquitous 5; Chris Fairclough Colour Library 21; Michael Freeman/Bruce Coleman Limited 27; Robert Harding Picture Library 11; Frank Lane Picture Agency 13, 15, 17; Luiz Claudio Margio /Bruce Coleman Limited 9; NASA/Science Photo Library 3; Panos Pictures 29; Zefa Picture Library 7, 23, 25.